Colourful
Days

FIRST EDITION
Series Editor Deborah Lock; **Senior Art Editor** Tory Gordon-Harris; **Design Assistant** Sadie Thomas;
Production Claire Pearson; **DTP Designer** Almudena Díaz; **Jacket Designer** Peter Radcliffe;
Reading Consultant Cliff Moon, M.Ed.

THIS EDITION
Editorial Management by Oriel Square
Produced for DK by WonderLab Group LLC
Jennifer Emmett, Erica Green, Kate Hale, *Founders*

Editors Grace Hill Smith, Libby Romero, Michaela Weglinski;
Photography Editors Kelley Miller, Annette Kiesow, Nicole DiMella;
Managing Editor Rachel Houghton; **Designers** Project Design Company;
Researcher Michelle Harris; **Copy Editor** Lori Merritt; **Indexer** Connie Binder; **Proofreader** Larry Shea;
Reading Specialist Dr. Jennifer Albro; **Curriculum Specialist** Elaine Larson

Published in Great Britain by Dorling Kindersley Limited
DK, One Embassy Gardens, 8 Viaduct Gardens, London, SW11 7BW

The authorised representative in the EEA is
Dorling Kindersley Verlag GmbH. Arnulfstr. 124,
80636 Munich, Germany

Copyright © 2023 Dorling Kindersley Limited
A Penguin Random House Company
10 9 8 7 6 5 4 3 2
002-333470-May/2023

A catalogue record for this book
is available from the British Library.
ISBN: 978-0-2415-9311-0

Printed and bound in China

The publisher would like to thank the following for their kind permission to reproduce their images:
a=above; c=centre; b=below; l=left; r=right; t=top; b/g=background

Shutterstock.com: Africa Studio 25t, Gunnerchu 4bc, Happy Hirtzel 26-27, Songdech Kothmongkol 11c

Cover images: *Front:* **Dreamstime.com:** Allegro7 cla, crb, Benchart, Raman Maisei cra;
Back: **Shutterstock.com:** Fantastic Day cla, robuart cra

All other images © Dorling Kindersley
For more information see: www.dkimages.com

For the curious
www.dk.com

Colourful Days

Elizabeth Hester

Come and play with me.

How many colours
can you see?

white

We can play
in the cold,
white snow.

We can look at
the purple flowers.

purple

We can run
around the trees
that have
pink blossoms.

pink

grey

We can play
with the small,
grey rabbits.

We can look
at the boats
on the blue sea.

blue

We can play
near the
tall, yellow
sunflowers.

yellow

orange

We can eat
a frozen orange
treat.

red

We can kick
the red leaves.
We can also pick
the red apples.

black

22

We can look
at the black ants.
We can see the
black beetle.

We can croak
like the small,
brown frogs.

 brown

We can walk past the tall, green trees.

green

We can hang up
silver balls and
put on gold crowns.

silver and gold

silver

gold

How many colours can you see?

Glossary

blue
the colour of some toy cars, blueberries, and the sea

green
the colour of pine trees, tree frogs, and some parrots

orange
the colour of pumpkins, carrots, and oranges

red
the colour of some leaves, apples, and holly berries

yellow
the colour of bananas, lemons, and sunflowers

Quiz

Answer the questions to see what you have learnt. Check your answers with an adult.

What colour is each of these things?

1. Some blossoms on trees in the spring

2. Some small, fuzzy rabbits

3. Some ants and beetles

4. Small frogs that blend in with leaves

5. A crown

1. Pink 2. Grey 3. Black 4. Brown or green 5. Gold